'IWA
The Hawaiian Legend

by
Dietrich Varez

Dedication

This book is dedicated to David and Christine Reed of Petroglyph Press who have helped me and many others to spread and make available the unique culture of Hawai'i.

Copyright 2015 by Dietrich Varez

DVarez.com

All rights reserved

No part of this book may be reproduced or transmitted in any form or by any means, electronic or mechanical, including photocopying, recording or by any information storage and retrieval system, without permission in writing from the author.

ISBN 978-0-912180-72-4

Published in Hilo, Hawai'i by Petroglyph Press, Ltd.
160 Kamehameha Avenue - Hilo, Hawai'i 96720
Phone (808) 935-6006 - Toll Free (888) 666-8644
PetroglyphPress@hawaiiantel.net
Facebook.com/PetroglyphHilo
www.PetroglyphPress.com

First Edition ~ April 2015

INTRODUCTION

The Hawaiian "Legend of 'Iwa" is unique for several reasons. First, it makes a moral statement against thievery. Then, the legend is linked to an actual historical person; namely the famous chief 'Umi who lived circa 1550 A.D. and ruled the island of Hawai'i. The legend also establishes a metaphorical link between the animal world and that of man. The protagonist 'Iwa exhibits and engages in the same traits as his namesake, the Great Frigatebird, notoriously known for its thievery. And further yet, for those who are fishermen, the Hawaiian method of catching octopus using a cowry shell lure, *lūhe'e* is explained and depicted.

The author's intent here is to retell the legend through explained illustrations rather than illustrated text. Therefore a few coordinations between the visual and textual needed to be made. The basic legend, however, remains the foundation of this story.

Dietrich Varez, 2015

At Halapē in Puna, on the island of Hawai'i, is where this story began. The old fisherman Kea'au had gone there to look for *leho*, cowry shells, from which to make lures for catching *he'e*, octopus. Cowries are a favorite of *he'e*, and are easy for them to see. The way the lures are fashioned makes them seem to *hula*, or dance, becoming irresistible to the *he'e*.

Corals and seashells all belong to the goddess Hina. Kea'au had respectfully asked her permission before beginning his search. He had draped a lei of seaweed, *limu kala*, over the sacred stone at the fishing shrine of Ku'ula, the god and protector of fishermen.

Kea'au was famed for his great skill in catching *he'e*. He was the best in all the islands. Halapē was his secret spot when searching for just the right shells.

That day he was wading along the shoreline looking under ledges and rolling rocks over to find the very best hidden *leho*.

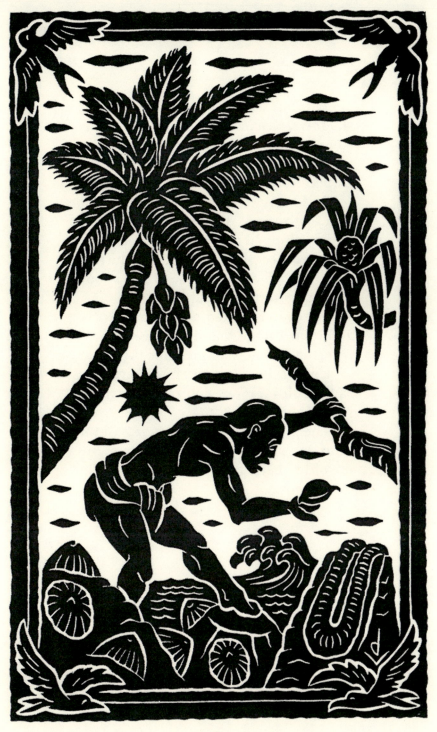

The sun was straight up and left no shadows. Kea'au rested in a small sandy cove by some big boulders enjoying some of the fat limpets, *'opihi,* he had gathered from the rocks.

Suddenly it became very still. The wind stopped. The waves stopped. Kea'au stopped chewing and looked behind and all around. Then he felt the first rumbling. The earth groaned and shook from a powerful earthquake.

The water sucked out from the cove and then a huge foaming wave rose up from the sea and slammed into the shore.

Kea'au clung to a nearby coconut tree as the rolling rocks and receding water pulled at him.

The great wave washed away all the sand and soil from around the tree, but the old fisherman held on tight.

Several sudden and jolting aftershocks followed. Kea'au saw a whole section of land slide into the sea. Only the quaking treetops were left visible above the water.

Just when Kea'au thought he too would be washed out to sea the quake stopped. The coconut tree which had saved him continued swaying even after Kea'au had let go. The old man thanked the tree for his life.

Near the tree, by a small outcropping of rocks where the sand had been washed away, a curious shape protruded from the rubble. It was made of wood and looked very old.

Amidst the debris and stranded fish old Kea'au carefully went for a closer look at the unusual artifact revealed by the wave.

"It's an old canoe," he said to himself. "Long ago someone secreted it away here in these rocks."

Kea'au cautiously crept closer. He was still nervous from the earthquake. He brushed away some of the debris. Then he saw what seemed to be a *kā wa'a*, a canoe bailer, tucked snugly up into the bow crevice of the old hulk.

Kea'au carefully pulled the concealed *kā wa'a* out. Inside of the bailer was a neat white *kapa* bundle tied with some braided red sennit cord. Kea'au could not take his eyes off it. What could it be?

As the old fisherman untied the red cord and opened the *kapa* there was another piece of wrapping inside. It was the precious *'ōūholowai kapa* that Ola'a was famous for, dyed and decorated differently on each side. Next there was a different piece of wrapping. It was the rare *eleuli kapa* that carried a soft scent. As Kea'au continued unwrapping the bundle he found another, four pieces in all.

Kea'au was entranced by the white packet. And as he removed the last piece of soft white *kapa* he was stunned to see the contents: two deep-red glowingly beautiful *leho*.

"*Leho 'ula*, red shells," he whispered to himself. The two *leho* were so very radiant that it was hard to look at them very long. He had to wrap the *kapa* back over them after a short while.

"These are not just ordinary *leho*," he thought. "Surely they are a gift sent by Hina herself." He noted too that the *leho* already had holes drilled into them by which they could be tied into an octopus lure, *lūhe'e*.

Without hesitation Kea'au reached for the small pouch he had tucked into his *malo*.

There by the seashore old Kea'au took out some strong *olonā* cord and a sharp pointed bone hook, *makau iwi*. He carefully tied the beautiful *leho 'ula* together around a flat stone. Then he added the hook and a short tassel of *kī* leaves to finish. The leaves made the lure dance for the *he'e*, who became so enticed they would wrap themselves around the *leho* and then the fisherman could set the hook.

"We shall see, we shall see," he mumbled to himself as he deftly made all the proper knots and twists for a well-fashioned *lūhe'e*. But Kea'au had barely finished tying the shells together when a very strange thing happened.

He'e came crawling out of the ocean from all directions. They had spotted the *leho 'ula* and were sliding over the shoreline rocks toward Kea'au and his glowing red *lūhe'e*.

Even 'Iwa, the Great Frigatebird, came by for a look at this special *lūhe'e* and Kea'au knew he must protect it from the thieving bird.

"In all my years of fishing I've never seen anything like this," thought old Kea'au in amazement.

"These must be magic shells. I've not even put them into the water and already there are more *he'e* than a whole village can eat."

He quickly covered up the *lūhe'e* in its *kapa* wrappings. Then he proceeded to gather together all of the *he'e*. There were so many that he had to make a rack on which to dry them in the sun. When they were all dry and well cured he bound them together and into bundles. Then he headed joyfully home to his village.

In the village, Kea'au excitedly told his family and neighbors of his adventure and showed everyone the radiant *leho 'ula*. He named the *lūhe'e* Kalokuna, and put it away in a secret place.

The people of Kea'au's village never went hungry. There were always plenty of *he'e* for eating and trading. Soon, the news of the fantastic *leho 'ula* of Kea'au spread over the entire island.

As was the rule in those days, all property belonged to the chiefs and could be confiscated from the people at any time. 'Umi, a famous high chief that ruled the island of Hawai'i, was at that time living in Kona. Before long he heard about Kea'au's wondrous red *lūhe'e*, Kalokuna.

'Umi became jealous and, coveting the special *leho 'ula*, he ordered the shells to be taken from Kea'au. The chief sent his guards to search Kea'au's village. They finally found the white *kapa* bundle tucked away in the rafters of the old fisherman's house.

The arrogant guards took the white *kapa* bundle and brought it to 'Umi. To make matters even worse, all the *he'e* left Puna and followed the *leho 'ula* to the Kona side of the island. Kea'au's village was left without their favorite source of food.

"We must try to get our *leho 'ula* back," said Kea'au. Together with the elders of the village he formed a plan to retrieve his famed Kalokuna from 'Umi. They resolved to hire a thief to steal it away from the chief.

Kea'au readied his *wa'a*, canoe, and filled it with gifts. Then he set off in search of a skilled thief. Throughout the districts of Puna, Ka'u and Kona he sought a thief smart enough to accomplish the task. He touched upon Kohala and traveled through Hāmākua and Hilo without finding his man.

Kea'au traveled on around Maui and Lāna'i to Moloka'i. There he met a man who told him that there was reported to be a very clever thief living at Mokukapu on the island of O'ahu. "Sail on until you pass Makapu'u and look for the *kukui* grove at Mokukapu. There you will find a clever thief named 'Iwa."

In those times people thought there was little wrong with thievery or stealing, getting caught at it was the crime. This thief named ʻIwa had never, ever been caught stealing. So, no one was even really sure he was a thief.

Keaʻau finally reached the grove of *kukui* trees at Mokukapu and wearily pulled his *waʻa* ashore.

"Where is the thief ʻIwa?" the old fisherman asked of some people there. But no one had heard of such a name.

Just as Keaʻau was about ready to give up his search for ʻIwa, a young boy suddenly appeared by the *waʻa*. It was ʻIwa. So stealthy was this ʻIwa no one had seen nor heard him coming.

"I am 'Iwa," said the boy. "I hope I didn't startle you. It's these new sandals," he excused himself. "They're a little too soft and quiet."

Kea'au was a bit surprised that the legendary thief was a mere boy, but he soon went on to explain about Kalokuna, the special *lūhe'e* and how the chief 'Umi had stolen it for himself and brought hardship to the village.

"We are asking you to regain these *leho 'ula* for us who rightfully own them. Will you help us?" asked Kea'au hopefully.

At first the boy seemed more interested in the gifts Kea'au had brought and was unashamedly probing around in the old man's *wa'a*. Eventually, with the irreverence of youth, he shrugged and agreed to help Kea'au and travel with him back to the island of Hawai'i.

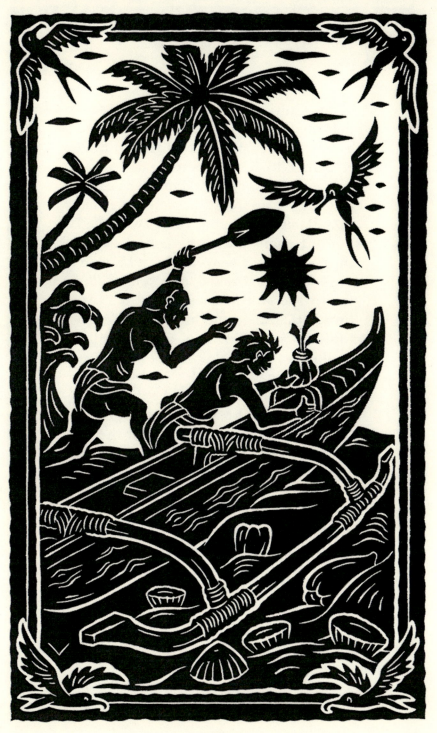

In addition to his soft and silent sandals made of *wauke* fiber, 'Iwa also had a magic *hoe*, canoe paddle, named Kapahi. With just four strokes of this *hoe* 'Iwa could row any *wa'a* to any island.

"You sit up front," he said to Kea'au. "I will take the stern." Then 'Iwa called out to Kapahi and with his first stroke they passed between Ni'ihau and Kaua'i. "Are we there?" asked 'Iwa. "Hawai'i is far to the south," said Kea'au. 'Iwa turned the canoe and his second stroke took them past O'ahu. On his third stroke they left Moloka'i and Lāna'i behind and floated between Molikini and Maui. With his fourth stroke they were gliding into the smooth waters of Keāhole, on the western side of the island of Hawai'i, where 'Umi was fishing from a large *wa'a*.

They could tell it was the royal *wa'a* because of the woven thatch awning which shaded the chief. 'Iwa and Kea'au did not let 'Umi see them approaching.

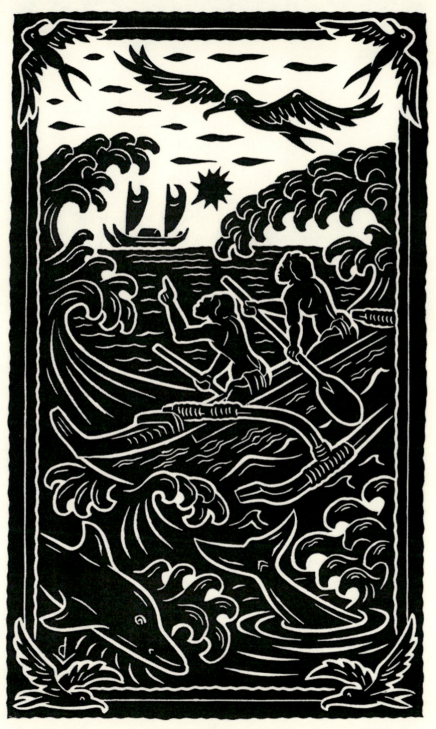

'Umi's huge fishing *wa'a* floated lazily in the calm Kona water. The chief was using the *lūhe'e* taken from Kea'au.

"Keep our *wa'a* here and out of sight," said 'Iwa, as he silently slipped into the water with the agility of a monk seal. He took a couple of very deep breaths and dove down to the bottom where he effortlessly walked on the sea floor until he reached the place the chief was fishing.

'Iwa swam up beneath 'Umi's *wa'a*. Then he followed the line from 'Umi's vessel to Kalokuna, which rested on the coral below. Even underwater, 'Iwa had to shield his eyes when he spotted the magical *lūhe'e*. He quickly untied it and then fastened the line to a coral head.

As 'Iwa worked down below, the rocking of the sea had soothed 'Umi into a gentle slumber. He was dozing above, suspecting nothing.

With the prize securely in his grasp 'Iwa swiftly and silently returned to his companion.

Back in the *wa'a* with Kea'au, 'Iwa gave the old fisherman the precious *leho 'ula*. Then he firmly gripped Kapahi and, calling out to his magic *hoe*, in just four strokes returned them to Kea'au's village at Leleiwi, a point of land between Hilo and Puna.

The *leho 'ula* were safely back. The people of the village rejoiced. Everyone praised 'Iwa and a great feast was held in his honor.

Meanwhile, at Keāhole, it did not take long for 'Umi to discover he was not able to pull up Kalokuna. After seeking in vain among his men for a diver who could go deep enough to untangle the line, he sent runners around the island to find a man who could hold his breath long enough to retrieve it. When they arrived at Leleiwi and found 'Iwa he boldly told them the story of how he had taken the *lūhe'e*. He was quickly summoned before chief 'Umi.

As thieves live only to steal, paying no heed to friendships or loyalties, 'Iwa was easily talked into stealing once more. That very night he went back to Kea'au's house and stole Kalokuna back for chief 'Umi.

Chief 'Umi was very impressed with 'Iwa's stealthy skills. "This 'Iwa could serve me well," thought 'Umi to himself. "I will test him further."

Chief 'Umi's most prized possession was the sacred stone club named Waipū. He kept the club in Pakaalana *heiau*, a sacred temple at Waipi'o Valley, guarded by two old women. A strong cord was tied between the necks of the two women and 'Umi's club hung dangling in the middle of the cord. The club was impossible to steal without rousing the women.

No one dared to go near the *heiau* or 'Umi's club because of the strict *kapu*. A special crier sounded the alert five times each night, warning the people not to be out. They were told to go to sleep. No dogs should bark nor roosters crow, and the pigs could not run loose.

"Let's see how good you really are," said 'Umi with a smirk to 'Iwa. "See if you can steal my club from the *heiau* and its guardians."

'Iwa agreed to the test. He was beginning to like 'Umi and the chief's eager patronage of his thievery.

As the sun was setting the clever 'Iwa swiftly ran to the *heiau* where the club was kept. He pretended to be the crier and shouted to the women.

"Where is the sacred club of 'Umi? Is it safe? Are you guarding it well? Let me touch it to see that it has not been stolen!"

The women were fooled by 'Iwa's false authority and let him put his hands on the club momentarily. In an instant 'Iwa jerked Waipū free of the cord and was gone from the *heiau*.

'Iwa could still hear the shouts and cries of the old women as he pretended to be asleep. No one had seen him at the *heiau*.

In the morning, after the chief's guards had searched the entire village for the sacred club, 'Iwa sauntered to Chief 'Umi's house. Everyone was in an uproar over the missing club and the unsuccessful search.

As 'Umi was questioning his guards he spied 'Iwa. "Here is a club I found last night," 'Iwa said innocently to the amazed 'Umi. "Perhaps it is yours. A sacred club such as this should be well guarded or one might find it missing," the boy added timidly.

'Umi had to swallow some of his pride. But he was not yet ready to admit defeat to this bold youth. Waipū was returned to the *heiau* and a new test of 'Iwa was readied.

'Umi was now obsessed with trying to outwit the boy. 'Iwa had caused him embarrassment by stealing Waipū from under the noses of his guards and the two old women guardians.

The chief called for six other noted thieves, one from each of the six districts on the island, to be matched against 'Iwa. Six against one! 'Umi gave the six men a house in which to store their stolen goods. He also gave 'Iwa a house in which to store his.

The thieves were given one night to perform the required task. Whichever of the two houses contained the most stolen goods by the next dawn would be the winner.

Darkness soon came and the villagers shut their houses. The six thieves plundered everything they could find. Soon their storehouse was filled to overflowing. 'Iwa was still at home and sound asleep.

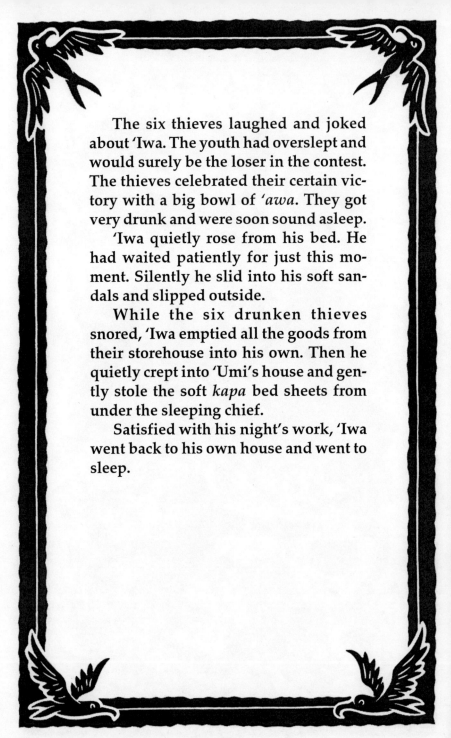

The six thieves laughed and joked about 'Iwa. The youth had overslept and would surely be the loser in the contest. The thieves celebrated their certain victory with a big bowl of *'awa*. They got very drunk and were soon sound asleep.

'Iwa quietly rose from his bed. He had waited patiently for just this moment. Silently he slid into his soft sandals and slipped outside.

While the six drunken thieves snored, 'Iwa emptied all the goods from their storehouse into his own. Then he quietly crept into 'Umi's house and gently stole the soft *kapa* bed sheets from under the sleeping chief.

Satisfied with his night's work, 'Iwa went back to his own house and went to sleep.

As the cool dawn came, 'Umi reached to pull his *kapa* sheets over himself but found them missing. Then he recalled the contest and went outside to check on his thieves.

When he arrived at the house of the six thieves they were sound asleep and he found nothing was stored there.

Then 'Umi went to 'Iwa's house. There was the boy also asleep on a huge pile of pilfered possessions.

The chief grinned when he recognized his own *kapa* bed sheet around the sleeping boy and trailing over his cache of loot.

He gently pulled the sheet up over the boy's shoulders and then went outside into the new day, smiling.

New problems were waiting just outside the door. The villagers were very upset over the theft of all their goods. They bitterly complained to chief 'Umi about 'Iwa and the thieves and all of the things they had stolen from the people.

It was then that Chief 'Umi realized the error of his ways. He had callously caused his people great concern and unhappiness by pursuing his petty games with 'Iwa.

'Umi went back into the house and woke 'Iwa up. When he had listened to the villagers' stories, the boy too could see the problems and misery caused by his thievery.

Together 'Umi and 'Iwa went outside the house and returned all the people's possessions. Then 'Umi gave everyone more than had been taken from them as a gesture of good will. He declared there would be no more stealing from then on.

'Iwa remained with chief 'Umi for some time after this. And it is said that 'Umi could not have become the great chief that he was without the occasional help of 'Iwa.

Eventually 'Iwa longed to go home to the *kukui* grove at Mokukapu. A grateful 'Umi stocked a huge double *wa'a* with gifts and provisions and 'Iwa set off for home with four strokes of his magic *hoe*, Kapahi.

There are many stories told of the great high chief 'Umi, who united the island of Hawai'i under his rule. It is said that he lived to be very old and that peace and prosperity abounded during his reign. A *heiau* known as Ahu a 'Umi was built on the saddle between the great mountains of Mauna Kea, Mauna Loa and Hualālai on Hawai'i island.

The old fisherman Kea'au and his village enjoyed the benefits of this peaceful time, even though they never saw the return of Kalokuna, the magical and precious *lūhe'e*.

That is the legend of 'Iwa and the *leho 'ula* of 'Umi and Kea'au. It is finished. The end. *Pau*.

GLOSSARY OF HAWAIIAN WORDS

'awa - a narcotic shrub *piper methisticum*
eleuli - rare scented kapa from 'Ōla'a, island of Hawai'i
Halapē - a land area in Puna district, island of Hawai'i
Hāmākua - northeast district, island of Hawai'i
he'e - octopus; to slide or surf
heiau - temple
Hina - a goddess of Hawai'i and Polynesia
Hilo - windward district, land section and village, island of Hawai'i
hoe - canoe paddle
hula – Hawaiian dance form
'Iwa - a legendary thief; Great Frigatebird, known for its thievery
Kalokuna - magical octopus lure; a variety of kalo; fresh water eel.
ka wa'a - canoe bailer
kapa - tapa, barkcloth made from plant fibers
kapu - taboo; forbidden; sacred
Kapahi - magic paddle; Lit. "To scatter the water"
Ka'u - southeast district, island of Hawai'i
Kaua'i - northernmost main island of Hawaiian chain
Kea'au - fisherman; a land section island of Hawai'i, Puna district
Keāhole - land section island of Hawai'i, Kona district; āhole fish
kī - tī, a plant, *cordyline terminalis*, with many practical uses
Kohala - northwest district, island of Hawai'i
Kona - leeward district, island of Hawai'i
kukui - candlenut tree

Ku'ula- god of fishermen; stone altar near the sea
Lāna'i - island near Maui
leho - cowry shell
leho 'ula - rare and highly prized red cowry shell
lei - floral decoration
Leleiwi - point of land between Hilo and Puna; Lit. bone altar
limu kala - a type of seaweed
lūhe'e - octopus lure
Makapu'u - eastern point on the island of O'ahu
makau iwi - bone hook
malo - male loincloth
Maui - second largest island; named after demi-god
Mokukapu - sacred land division, Kailua, island of O'ahu
Moloka'i - island, in legend the child of Hina
Molokini - islet off the island of Maui
Ni'ihau - small island near Kaua'i
O'ahu - most populous Hawaiian island
'Ōla'a - village and land section in Puna
olonā - shrub used for cord making
'opihi - limpet, a favorite food of Hawaiians
'ōūholowai - kapa made from mamaki bark, dyed differently on each side, special to 'Ōla'a, island of Hawai'i
Pakaalana - temple in Waipi'o Valley
pau - finished, ended, completed
Puna - land section, southeast Hawai'i island
'Umi- famous Hawaiian chief circa A.D. 1550
wa'a - canoe
Waipi'o Valley - land section, northeast island of Hawai'i
Waipū - legendary club of 'Umi
wauke - paper mulberry, used to make kapa

BIBLIOGRAPHY

Buck, Peter (Te Rangi Hiroa) *Arts & Crafts of Hawaii, Vol. VII Fishing*, 1964, B.P. Bishop Museum, Honolulu, Hawaii

Elbert, Samuel H., Editor, *Selections from Fornander's Hawaiian Antiquities and Folk-Lore*, 1959, UH Press, Honolulu, Hawaii

Kamakau, Samuel, *The Works of the People of Old*, 1976, Bishop Museum Press, Honolulu, Hawaii

Malo, David, *Hawaiian Antiquities, Translated from the Hawaiian* by Dr. Nathaniel Emerson,1898, 1951, B.P. Bishop Museum, Honolulu, Hawaii

Pukui, Mary Kawena and Samuel H. Elbert, *Hawaiian Dictionary*, 1986, UH Press, Honolulu, Hawaii

Pukui, Mary Kawena and Samuel H. Elbert, *Place Names of Hawaii*, 1974, UH Press, Honolulu, Hawaii

Westervelt, W.D., *Hawaiian Legends of Old Honolulu*, 1915, Reprint 1963, Charles E. Tuttle Co., Rutland, Vermont

Wight, Kahikāhealani, *Illustrated Hawaiian Dictionary*, 2005, Bess Press, Honolulu, Hawaii

About the Author

Dietrich Varez finds inspiration for his art from Hawaiian folklore and the natural beauty of the native 'ōhi'a forest surrounding his home in Volcano, Hawai'i. His original prints are each individually created, hand-cut and produced by the artist himself in his own matchless style. A prolific and unconventional printmaker, Varez believes in making his art available to a broad, popular audience, by pricing his work so anyone can afford a hand printed, signed piece of art. Although he has had no formal art training, he has been creating his unique form of block prints since moving to Volcano and finding rich inspiration in the realm of Pele. Varez is further exploring his creativity with full color paintings in oil. Visit www.DVarez.com for biographical information and a broad selection of his artwork, both block prints and full color prints. His work is available at the Volcano Art Center, Honolulu Museum of Art, Bishop Museum and Kōke'e Museum. Look for his signature artwork in the Reyn Spooner line of Hawaiian clothing.

Dietrich Varez was born in Berlin, Germany in 1939. He has made his home in Hawai'i since the age of eight, when his mother, Ursula married Manuel Varez, an American soldier who adopted her two sons and brought the family home to Hawai'i. Growing up island style on O'ahu, he attended the University of Hawai'i at Mānoa, earning a Masters degree in English. It was there he met his wife, Linda, a fellow artist, before moving the family to Hawai'i Island in 1968.

HINA, The Goddess and *Pele and Hi'iaka, A Tale of Two Sisters* by Dietrich Varez are also published by Petroglyph Press.

Books published by PETROGLYPH PRESS

A CONCISE HISTORY OF THE HAWAIIAN ISLANDS
by Phil K. Barnes, Ph.D.
HILO LEGENDS
by Frances Reed
HINA - THE GODDESS
by Dietrich Varez
HOW TO USE HAWAIIAN FRUIT
by Agnes Alexander
'IWA, The Hawaiian Legend
by Dietrich Varez
JOYS OF HAWAIIAN COOKING
by Martin & Judy Beeman
THE KAHUNA, Versatile Masters of Old Hawai'i
by Likeke R. McBride
KONA LEGENDS
by Eliza D. Maguire
LEAVES FROM A GRASS HOUSE
by Don Blanding
PARADISE LOOT
by Don Blanding
PELE AND HI'IAKA, A Tale of Two Sisters
by Dietrich Varez
PETROGLYPHS OF HAWAI'I
by Likeke R. McBride
PLANTS OF HAWAII - HOW TO GROW THEM
by Fortunato Teho
PRACTICAL FOLK MEDICINE OF HAWAI'I
by Likeke R. McBride
STARS OVER HAWAI'I
by E. H. Bryan, Jr. and Richard Crowe, Ph.D.
THE STORY OF LAUHALA
by Edna W. Stall
**TROPICAL ORGANIC GARDENING
HAWAIIAN STYLE**
by Richard L. Stevens